IN HOSPITAL

BY

WILLIAM ERNEST HENLEY

British Library Cataloguing-in-Publication Data
A catalogue record for this book is available from the
British Library

William Ernest Henley

William Ernest Henley was born on 23rd August 1849, in Gloucester, England.

He attended Crypt Grammar School in Gloucester where the poet, scholar, and theologian, T. E. Brown, was headmaster. Brown had a made a huge impression on the young Henley and the two struck up a lifelong friendship. Henley claimed Brown to be "a man of Genius – the first I'd ever seen", and upon Brown's death in 1897, Henley wrote an admiring obituary to him in the *New Review*.

From the age of 12, Henley suffered from tuberculosis of the bone which eventually resulted in his left leg having to be amputated below the knee. According to Robert Louis Stevenson's letters, the character of Long John Silver was inspired by his friend Henley.

In 1867, Henley passed the Oxford Local Schools Examination and set off to London to establish himself as a journalist. Unfortunately, his career was frequently interrupted by long stays in hospital due to a diseased right foot which he refused to have amputated. During a three year stay at the Royal Infirmary of Edinburgh, Henley wrote and published his collection of poetry *In Hospital* (1875). This publication is noteworthy in particular for being some of the earliest examples of free verse written in England.

Henley married Hannah (Anna) Johnson Boyle on 22nd January 1878. The couple had one daughter together, Margaret, who died at the age of five and is reportedly the source of the name Wendy in J. M. Barrie's *Peter Pan*. Apparently she used to call Barrie her "fwendy wendy", resulting in the use of the name in the children's classic.

Henley's best-remembered work is his poem "Invictus", written in 1888. It is a passionate and defiant poem, reportedly written as a demonstration of resilience following the amputation of his leg. This poem was famously recited to fellow inmates at Robben Island prison by Nelson Mandela to spread the message of empowerment and self-mastery. He also wrote a notable work of literary criticisms, *Views and Reviews,* in 1890, in which he covered a wide range of works by prominent authors.

Henley died of tuberculosis in 1903 at the age of 53 at his home in Woking, and his ashes were interred in his daughter's grave in the churchyard at Cockayne Hatley in Bedfordshire, England.

I

THE morning mists still haunt the stony street;
The northern summer air is shrill and cold;
And lo, the Hospital, grey, quiet, old,
Where Life and Death like friendly chafferers meet.
Thro' the loud spaciousness and draughty gloom
A small, strange child — o aged yet so young! —
Her little arm besplinted and beslung,
Precedes me gravely to the waiting-room.
I limp behind, my confidence all gone.
The grey-haired soldier-porter waves me on,
And on I crawl, and still my spirits fail:
tragic meanness seems so to environ
These corridors and stairs of stone and iron,
Cold, naked, clean — half-workhouse and half jail.

II

A SQUARE:, squat room (a cellar on promotion),
Drab to the soul, drab to the very daylight;
Plasters astray in unnaturallooking tinware;
Scissors and lint and apothecary's jars.

Here, on a bench a skeleton would writhe from,
Angry and sore, I wait to be admitted:
Wait till my heart is lead upon my stomach,
While at their ease two dressers do their chores.

One has a probe — it feels to me a crowbar.
A small boy sniffs and shudders after bluestone.
A poor old tramp explains his poor old ulcers.
Life is (I think) a blunder and a shame.

III

THE gaunt brown walls
Look infinite in their decent meanness.
There is nothing of home in the noisy kettle,
The fulsome fire.

The atmosphere
Suggests the trail of a ghostly druggist.
Dressings and lint on the long, lean table —
Whom are they for?

The patients yawn,
Or lie as in training for shroud and coffin.

A nurse in the corridor scolds and wrangles.
It's grim and strange.

Far footfalls clank.
The bad burn waits with his head unbandaged.
My neighbour chokes in the clutch of chloral . . .
O, a gruesome world!

IV

Behold me waiting — waiting for the knife.
A little while, and at a leap I storm
The thick, sweet mystery of chloroform,
The drunken dark, the little death-in-life.
The gods are good to me: I have no wife,
No innocent child, to think of as I near
The fateful minute; nothing all-too dear
Unmans me for my bout of passive strife.
Yet am I tremulous and a trifle sick,
And, face to face with chance, I shrink a little:
My hopes are strong, my will is something weak.
Here comes the basket? Thank you. I am ready.
But, gentlemen my porters, life is brittle:
You carry Caesar and his fortunes — steady!

V

You are carried in a basket,
Like a carcase from the shambles,
To the theatre, a cockpit
Where they stretch you on a table.

Then they bid you close your eyelids,
And they mask you with a napkin,
And the anæsthetic reaches
Hot and subtle through your being.

And you gasp and reel and shudder
In a rushing, swaying rapture,
While the voices at your elbow
Fade — receding — fainter — farther.

Lights about you shower and tumble,
And your blood seems crystallising —
Edged and vibrant, yet within you
Racked and hurried back and forward.

Then the lights grow fast and furious,
And you hear a noise of waters,
And you wrestle, blind and dizzy,
In an agony of effort,

Till a sudden lull accepts you,
And you sound an utter darkness . . .
And awaken . . . with a struggle . . .
On a hushed, attentive audience.

VI

LIKE as a flamelet blanketed in smoke,
So through the anæsthetic shows my life;
So flashes and so fades my thought, at strife
With the strong stupor that I heave and choke
And sicken at, it is so foully sweet.
Faces look strange from space — and disappear.
Far voices, sudden loud, offend my ear —
And hush as sudden. Then my senses fleet:
All were a blank, save for this dull, new pain
That grinds my leg and foot; and brokenly
Time and the place glimpse on to me again;
And, unsurprised, out of uncertainty,
I wake — relapsing — somewhat faint and fain,
To an immense, complacent dreamery.

VII

LIVED on one's back,
In the long hours of repose
Life is a practical nightmare —
Hideous asleep or awake.

Shoulders and loins
Ache - - - !
Ache, and the mattress,
Run into boulders and hummocks,
Glows like a kiln, while the bedclothes —
Tumbling, importunate, daft —
Ramble and roll, and the gas,
Screwed to its lowermost,
An inevitable atom of light,
Haunts, and a stentorous sleeper
Snores me to hate and despair.

All the old time
Surges malignant before me;
Old voices, old kisses, old songs
Blossom derisive about me;
While the new days
Pass me in endless procession:
A pageant of shadows

In Hospital

Silently, leeringly wending
On . . . and still on . . . still on!

Far in the stillness a cat
Languishes loudly. A cinder
Falls, and the shadows
Lurch to the leap of the flame. The next man to me
Turns with a moan; and the snorer,
The drug like a rope at his throat,
Gasps, gurgles, snorts himself free, as the night-nurse,
Noiseless and strange,
Her bull's eye half-lanterned in apron,
(Whispering me, 'Are ye no sleepin' yet?
Passes, list-slippered and peering,
Round . . . and is gone.

Sleep comes at last —
Sleep full of dreams and misgivings —
Broken with brutal and sordid
Voices and sounds that impose on me,
Ere I can wake to it,
The unnatural, intolerable day.

9

VIII

THE greater masters of the commonplace,
REMBRANDT and good SIR WALTER — only these
Could paint her all to you: experienced ease
And antique liveliness and ponderous grace;
The sweet old roses of her sunken face;
The depth and malice of her sly, grey eyes;
The broad Scots tongue that flatters, scolds, defies,
The thick Scots wit that fells you like a mace.
These thirty years has she been nursing here,
Some of them under SYME, her hero still.
Much is she worth, and even more is made of her.
Patients and students hold her very dear.
The doctors love her, tease her, use her skill.
They say ' The Chief' himself is half-afraid of her.

IX

SOME three, or five, or seven, and thirty years;
A Roman nose; a dimpling double-chin;
Dark eyes and shy that, ignorant of sin,
Are yet acquainted, it would seem, with tears;
A comely shape; a slim, high-coloured hand,

Graced, rather oddly, with a signet ring;
A bashful air, becoming everything;
A well-bred silence always at command.
Her plain print gown, prim cap, and bright steel chain
Look out of place on her, and I remain
Absorbed in her, as in a pleasant mystery.
Quick, skilful, quiet, soft in speech and touch . . .
'Do you like nursing?' 'Yes, Sir, very much.'
Somehow, I rather think she has a history.

X

BLUE-EYED and bright of face but waning fast
Into the sere of virginal decay,
I view her as she enters, day by day,
As a sweet sunset almost overpast.
Kindly and calm, patrician to the last,
Superbly falls her gown of sober gray,
And on her chignon's elegant array
The plainest cap is somehow touched with caste.
She talks BEETHOVEN; frowns disapprobation
At BALZAC'S name, sighs it at 'poor GEORGE
SAND'S';
Knows that she has exceeding pretty hands;
Speaks Latin with a right accentuation;

And gives at need (as one who understands)
Draught, counsel, diagnosis, exhortation.

XI

HIST ? . . .
Through the corridor's echoes
Louder and nearer
Comes a great shuffling of feet.
Quick, every one of you,
Staighten your quilts, and be decent!
Here's the Professor.

In he comes first
With the bright look we know,
From the broad, white brows the kind eyes
Soothing yet nerving you. Here at his elbow,
White-capped, white-aproned, the Nurse,
Towel on arm and her inkstand
Fretful with quills.
Here in the ruck, anyhow,
Surging along,
Louts, duffers, exquisites, students, and prigs —
Whiskers and foreheads, scarf-pins and spectacles —
Hustles the Class! And they ring themselves

In Hospital

Round the first bed, where the Chief
(His dressers and clerks at attention),
Bends in inspection already.

So shows the ring
Seen from behind round a conjurer
Doing his pitch in the street.
High shoulders, low shoulders, broad shoulders,
narrow ones,
Round, square, and angular, serry and shove;
While from within a voice,
Gravely and weightily fluent,
Sounds; and then ceases; and suddenly
(Look at the stress of the shoulders!)
Out of a quiver of silence,
Over the hiss of the spray,
Comes a low cry, and the sound
Of breath quick intaken through teeth
Clenched in resolve. And the Master
Breaks from the crowd, and goes,
Wiping his hands.
To the next bed, with his pupils
Flocking and whispering behind him.

Now one can see.
Case Number One

Sits (rather pale) with his bedclothes
Stripped up, and showing his foot
(Alas for God's Image!)
Swaddled in wet, white lint
Brilliantly hideous with red.

XII

Two and thirty is the ploughman.
He's a man of gallant inches,
And his hair is close and curly,
And his beard;
But his face is wan and sunken,
And his eyes are large and brilliant,
And his shoulder-blades are sharp,
And his knees.

He is weak of wits, religious,
Full of sentiment and yearning,
Gentle, faded — with a cough
And a snore.
When his wife (who was a widow,
And is many years his elder)
Fails to write, and that is always,
He desponds.

Let his melancholy wander,
And he'll tell you pretty stories
Of the women that have wooed him
Long ago;
Or he'll sing of bonnie lasses
Keeping sheep among the heather,
With a crackling, hackling click
In his voice

XIII

As with varnish red and glistening
Dripped his hair; his feet looked rigid;
Raised, he settled stiffly sideways:
You could see his hurts were spinal.

He had fallen from an engine,
And been dragged along the metals.
It was hopeless, and they knew it;
So they covered him, and left him.

As he lay, by fits half sentient,
Inarticulately moaning,
With his stockinged soles protruded
Stark and awkward from the blankets,

To his bed there came a woman,
Stood and looked and sighed a little,
And departed without speaking,
As himself a few hours after.

I was told it was his sweetheart.
They were on the eve of marriage.
She was quiet as a statue,
But her lip was grey and writhen.

XIV

FROM the winter's grey despair,
From the summer's golden languor,
Death, the lover of Life,
Frees us for ever.

Inevitable, silent, unseen,
Everywhere always,
Shadow by night and as light in the day,
Signs she at last to her chosen;
And, as she waves them forth,
Sorrow and Joy
Lay by their looks and their voices,

Set down their hopes, and are made
One in the dim Forever.

Into the winter's grey delight,
Into the summer's golden dream,
Holy and high and impartial,
Death, the mother of Life,
Mingles all men for ever.

XV

HIs brow spreads large and placid, and his eye
Is deep and bright, with steady looks that still.
Soft lines of tranquil thought his face fulfill —
His face at once benign and proud and shy.
If envy scout, if ignorance deny,
His faultless patience, his unyielding will,
Beautiful gentleness and splendid skill,
Innumerable gratitudes reply.
His wise, rare smile is sweet with certaintity
And seems in all his patients to compel
Such love and faith as failure cannot quell
We hold him for another Herakles,
Battling with custom, prejudice, disease,
As once the son of Zeus with Death and Hell.

XVI

EXCEEDING tall, but built so well his height
Half-disappears in flow of chest and limb;
Moustache and whisker trooper-like in trim;
Frank-faced, frank-eyed, frank-hearted; always bright
And always punctual — morning, noon, and night;
Bland as a Jesuit, sober as a hymn;
Humorous, and yet without a touch of whim;
Gentle and amiable, yet full of fight.
His piety, though fresh and true in strain,
Has not yet whitewashed up his common mood
To the dead blank of his particular Schism.
Sweet, unaggressive, tolerant, most humane,
Wild artists like his kindly elderhood,
And cultivate his mild Philistinism.

XVII

O, THE fun, the fun and frolic
That The Wind that Shakes the Barley
Scatters through a penny-whistle
Tickled with artistic fingers!

In Hospital

Kate the scrubber (forty summers,
Stout but sportive) treads a measure,
Grinning, in herself a ballet,
Fixed as fate upon her audience.

Stumps are shaking, crutch-supported;
Splinted fingers tap the rhythm;
And a head all helmed with plasters
Wags a measured approbation.

Of their mattresslife oblivious,
All the patients, brisk and cheerful,
Are encouraging the dancer,
And applauding the musician.

Dim the gas-lights in the output
Of so many ardent smokers,
Full of shadow lurch the corners,
And the doctor peeps and passes.

There are, maybe, some suspicions
Of an alcoholic presence . . .
' Tak' a sup of this, my wumman! . . .
New Year comes but once a twelvemonth.

In Hospital

XVIII

Here, in this dim, dull, double-bedded room,
I play the father to a brace of boys,
Ailing but apt for every sort of noise,
Bedfast but brilliant yet with health and bloom.
Roden, the Irishman, is 'sieven past,'
Blue-eyed, snub-nosed, chubby, and fair of face.
Willie's but six, and seems to like the place,
A cheerful little collier to the last.
They eat, and laugh and sing, and fight, all day;
All night they sleep like dormice. See them play
At operations — Roden, the Professor,
Saws, lectures, takes the artery up, and ties;
Willie, self-chloroformed, with half-shut eyes,
Holding the limb and moaning — Case and Dresser.

XIX

SHE's tall and gaunt, and in her hard, sad face
With flashes of the old fun's animation
There lowers the fixed and peevish resignation
Bred of a past where troubles came apace,
She tells me that her husband, ere he died,
Saw seven of their children pass away,

20

And never knew the little lass at play
Out on the green, in whom, he's deified.
Her kin dispersed, her friends forgot and gone,
All simple faith her honest Irish mind,
Scolding her spoiled young saint, she labours on
Telling her dreams, taking her patients' part,
Trailing her coat sometimes: and you shall find
No rougher, quainter speech, nor kinder heart.

XX

HER little face is like a walnut shell
With wrinkling lines; her soft, white hair adorns
Her withered brows in quaint, straight curls, like
horns;
And all about her clings an old, sweet smell.
Prim is her gown and quakerlike her shawl.
Well might her bonnets have been born on her.
Can you conceive a Fairy Godmother
The subject of a strong religious call?
In snow or shine, from bed to bed she runs,
All twinkling smiles and texts and pious tales,
Her mittened hands, that ever give or pray,
Bearing a sheaf of tracts, a bag of buns:

In Hospital

A wee old maid that sweeps the Bridegroom's way,
Strong in a cheerful trust that never fails.

XXI

'TALK of pluck!' pursued the Sailor,
Set at euchre on his elbow,
'I was on the wharf at Charleston,
Just ashore from off the runner.

'It was grey and dirty weather,
And I heard a drum go rolling,
Rub-a-dubbing in the distance,
Awful dourlike and defiant.

'In and out among the cotton,
Mud, and chains, and stores, and anchors,
Tramped a squad of battered scarecrows —
Poor old Dixie's bottom dollar!

'Some had shoes, but all had rifles,
Them that wasn't bald was beardless,
And the drum was rolling Dixie,
And they stepped to it like men, sir!

'Rags and tatters, belts and bayonets,
On they swung, the drum a-rolling,
Mum and sour. It looked like fighting,
And they meant it too, by thunder!'

XXII

IT'S the Spring.
Earth has conceived, and her bosom,
Teeming with summer, is glad.

Vistas of change and adventure,
Thro' the green land
The grey roads go beckoning and winding,
Peopled with wains, and melodious
With harness-bells jangling:
Jangling and twangling rough rhythms
To the slow march of the stately, great horses
Whistled and shouted along.

White fleets of cloud,
Argosies heavy with fruitfulness,
Sail the blue peacefully. Green flame the hedgerows.
Blackbirds are bugling, and white in wet winds
Sway the tall poplars.

Pageants of colour and fragrance,
Pass the sweet meadows, and viewless
Walks the mild spirit of May,
Visibly blessing the world.

O, the brilliance of blossoming orchards!
O, the savour and thrill of the woods,
When their leafage is stirred
By the flight of the Angel of Rain!
Loud lows the steer; in the fallows
Rooks are alert; and the books
Gurgle and tinkle and trill. Thro' the gloamings,
Under the rare, shy stars,
Boy and girl wander
Dreaming in darkness and dew.

It's the Spring.
A sprightliness feeble and squalid
Wakes in the ward, and I sicken,
Impotent, winter at heart.

XXIII

DOWN the quiet eve,
Thro' my window with the sunset

In Hospital

Pipes to me a distant organ
Foolish ditties;

And, as when you change
Pictures in a magic lantern,
Books, beds, bottles, floor, and ceiling
Fade and vanish,

And I'm well once more....
August flares adust and torrid,
But my heart is full of April
Sap and sweetness.

In the quiet eve
I am loitering, longing, dreaming . . .
Dreaming, and a distant organ
Pipes me ditties.

I can see the shop,
I can smell the sprinkled pavement,
Where she serves — her chestnut chignon
Thrills my senses!

O, the sight and scent,
Wistful eve and perfumed pavement!
In the distance pipes an organ . . . The sensation

Comes to me anew,
And my spirit for a moment
Thro' the music breathes the blessed
Airs of London.

XXIV

STARING corpselike at the ceiling,
See his harsh, unrazored features,
Ghastly brown against the pillow,
And his throat so strangely bandaged!

Lack of work and lack of victuals,
A debauch of smuggled whisky,
And his children in the workhouse
Made the world so black a riddle

That he plunged for a solution;
And, although his knife was edgeless,
He was sinking fast towards one,
When they came, and found, and saved him.

Stupid now with shame and sorrow,
In the night I hear him sobbing.

But sometimes he talks a little.
He has told me all his troubles.

In his broad face, tanned and bloodless,
White and wild his eyeballs glisten;
And his smile, occult and tragic,
Yet so slavish, makes you shudder!

XXV

THIN-LEGGED, thin-chested, slight unspeakably,
Neat-footed and weak-fingered: in his face —
Lean, large-boned, curved of beak, and touched with race,
Bold-lipped, rich-tinted, mutable as the sea,
The brown eyes radiant with vivacity —
There shines a brilliant and romantic grace,
A spirit intense and rare, with trace on trace
Of passion and impudence and energy.
Valiant in velvet, light in ragged luck,
Most vain, most generous, sternly critical,
Buffoon and poet, lover and sensualist:
A deal of Ariel, just a streak of Puck,
Much Antony, of Hamlet most of all,
And something of the Shorter-Catechist.

XXVI

LAUGHS the happy April morn
Thro' my grimy, little window,
And a shaft of sunshine pushes
Thro' the shadows in the square.

Dogs are tracing thro' the grass,
Crows are cawing round the chimneys,
In and out among the washing
Goes the West at hide-and-seek.

Loud and cheerful clangs the bell
Here the nurses troop to breakfast.
Handsome, ugly, all are women . . .
O, the Spring — the Spring — the Spring!

XXVII

AT the barren heart of midnight,
When the shadow shuts and opens
As the loud flames pulse and flutter,
I can hear a cistern leaking.

Dripping, dropping, in a rhythm,
Rough, unequal, half-melodious,
Like the measures aped from nature
In the infancy of music;

Like the buzzing of an insect,
Still, irrational, persistent.
I must listen, listen, listen
In a passion of attention;

Till it taps upon my heartstrings,
And my very life goes dripping,
Dropping, dripping, drip-drip-dropping,
In the drip-drop of the cistern.

XXVIII

CARRY me out
Into the wind and the sunshine,
Into the beautiful world.

O, the wonder, the spell of the streets
The stature and strength of the horses
The rustle and echo of footfalls,
The flat roar and rattle of wheels!

In Hospital

A swift tram floats huge on us . . .
It's a dream?
The smell of the mud in my nostrils
Blows brave — like a breath of the sea!

As of old,
Ambulant, undulant drapery,
  Vaguely and strangely provocative,
Flutters and beckons. O, yonder —
Is it? — the gleam of a stocking!
Sudden, a spire

Wedged in the mist! O, the houses,
The long lines of lofty, grey houses,
Cross-hatched with shadow and light!
These are the streets....
Each is an avenue leading
Whither I will!

Free . . .!
Dizzy, hysterical, faint,
I sit, and the carriage rolls on with me
Into the wonderful world.

THE OLD INFIRMARY, EDINBURGH, 1873-75

Lightning Source UK Ltd.
Milton Keynes UK
UKOW04f1049290917
310112UK00002B/389/P

9 781473 322486